devils let loose

The Story of the Lincoln Riots, 1911

Written by Pat Nurse
Historical Research by Tony Gadd

ISBN N° 1 903172 13 6

Published by Barny Books, Hough on the Hill, Grantham, Lincolnshire
Produced by TUCANNdesign&print, 19 High Street, Heighington, Lincoln LN4 1RG
Tel & Fax: 01522 790009 www.tucann.co.uk

“And diff’ring judgements serve but to declare
That truth lies somewhere, if we knew but where.”

- Cowper

INTRODUCTION

Chaos, damage and blood-stained streets greeted the people of Lincoln on the morning of August 20, 1911, after two shameful nights of rioting. Almost 90 years later these exceptional events in history are all but forgotten.

Perhaps it's because the story does not stand out as one of the City's finest. Those who should have taken a strong lead in maintaining order or offering support and direction were at best inefficient and at worst downright incompetent.

The police couldn't distinguish between the innocent and the guilty as they "cracked heads like walnuts" in a desperate attempt to protect themselves and gain control, and the magistrates failed to turn up to support the military and restore order. The City's first citizen was away on holiday and wouldn't come home despite the fact that as Mayor and chairman of the bench, he should have been here. And the public – 5000 strong against a handful of police officers – acted as "devils let loose" stoning and beating anyone or anything in sight just because there was no-one to stop them.

Even though 12 men were eventually singled out for judgement, compared to today's legal standards the question must be asked whether justice was done.

Lack of historical documentation has probably prevented the story from being told before. Some papers remained in the hands of Special Branch until a request was made for them to be transferred to the archives in 1994.

Others, which should have been stored, were saved from the incinerator at a Lincoln tip by a character named "Rabbits." A former resident in Shakespeare Street, Lincoln, until his death, he searched through local rubbish looking for items of "value" that he could either sell or barter. It was sometime in the late 1960s or early 1970s that he approached local historian Tony Gadd in the pub with a battered grey box containing information which was held together with rusty, old paperclips. Had this not been found this important story might well have been buried forever.

How these important documents - which include telegrams from the then Home Secretary Winston Churchill - ended up where they did is a matter of pure speculation so many years on. A cynic might say they were so damning on the authorities at the time that they were glad to be rid of them. Others might say their importance was simply overlooked, or they got lost, during times of reorganisation for the local authorities, city boundaries and the courts and police services during the last 90 years.

Whatever the truth of the situation, this is a story that must be recorded not only for posterity, but also in fairness to those who shouldered the blame at a time when scapegoats had to be found to satisfy the demands of the ratepayers.

It is dedicated to police officer and firefighter Alfred Clay and local tradesman Mr T.H Starmer who both lost their lives during this most turbulent time in Lincoln's history.

PAT NURSE, Lincoln, 18th February 2001

Railway Crossing, High Street, Lincoln early 1900s

Acknowledgements

The Public Record Office, Kew (Pages 58, 59 and 63 to 67)

Lincolnshire Police Museum at the Museum of Lincolnshire Life (Pages 23 and 29)

The Lincolnshire Library Service

Maurice Hodson (Page 41)

Lincolnshire Fire & Rescue Service and Lincolnshire Police (Page 5)

Friends & Relatives of Tony & Pat

LINCOLNSHIRE

POLICE & FIRE and RESCUE

CHIEF OFFICERS

COMMENDATION

Presented to the family of

POLICE CONSTABLE/FIREMAN ALFRED CLAY

In recognition of his actions at a fire at

OSBOURNE'S MOTOR WORKS
PRINCESS STREET - LINCOLN

on

24th AUGUST 1911

CITATION

On 24th August 1911 whilst carrying out his duties at a fire at Osbourne's Motor Works, Princess Street, Lincoln, Police Constable/Fireman Alfred Clay sadly met his death.

After the successful damping down of the fire, the building was left in an imminent state of collapse. Alfred Clay was keeping a large crowd from surging underneath the unstable wall, when without warning it collapsed upon him. He was pulled from the debris but unfortunately died whilst being attended by the Doctor.

With little regard for his personal safety, Alfred Clay's courageous efforts undoubtedly saved many from fatal injury. The actions of Police Constable/Fireman Alfred Clay were of the highest order and in the very best traditions of the Police and Fire Services.

Chief Constable

Chief Fire Officer

Commendation Posthumously awarded to Alfred Clay after his heroic story emerged while researching for this book

CHAPTER ONE
"CLEAR THE CROSSING!"

AUGUST 18, 1911. Great Northern Level Crossing, High Street. 9.30pm - 1am.

Police must have felt the tension building up all day. They were guarding the Railway Crossing gates by order of Home Secretary Winston Churchill. A national railway strike had been declared and trouble was expected in Lincoln.

Attempts by workers to entice the guards away from their post failed, but supporters from the Boilermakers' Union, which was also on strike, had joined the few pickets all day to help them stop the trains. Despite their efforts, the railway company's service was still running.

By 9.30pm, people merged into a large crowd of some thousands adding weight and strength to the cause. Their overwhelming presence blocked the roadway and gates.

At 9.45pm, the delayed passenger train from Doncaster began to shunt over Brayford Bridge. It had no choice but to pull up short of the gates. The Grantham train was waiting to cross from the opposite direction.

The signalman had warned the gateman by bell that trains were on their way but every effort they made to open the gates was resisted by the weight of numbers now estimated at 5,000 people.

Tramcars north and south of the crossing were held up and used as excellent vantage points by people who were obviously excited by what was unfolding before them. Onlookers began to congregate on the footbridge over the railway. The doorways and windows of the Great Northern Hotel were thick with spectators.

Matters remained in a peaceful state until the relief of police came on duty at 10pm led by Chief Constable John Thomas Coleman. Boos and derisive cheers greeted him. There was already much hostility towards Coleman. A few days earlier, on August 14, he had ordered that the Boilermakers Union banner be torn down during a labour demonstration in the City Centre.

Within a few minutes of arriving at the scene on High Street, Chief Coleman gave the order to police to draw their truncheons and charge to clear the crossing at any cost. This surprised the crowd and held it still and silent for a moment but it proved to be the spark that ignited the blaze.

Hooting sounds broke out as police moved forward to open the gates. One was swung wide, but if Chief Coleman thought the police were now in control, he would soon learn that the battle was not going to be easily won.

The gate was immediately banged shut again by the crowd on the north side of the crossing. People damned Coleman and "all his works."

Five constables with batons walked in front of the gates and this show of force proved sufficient to hold the crowd back but then people hurled bricks at the signal box. A cheer greeted the assault and pandemonium followed. Missiles fired from catapults crashed through the panes of the box. The signalman was driven by sheer force from his post.

It looked as if the trains would be stranded but a "plucky boy" named Schofield, a young railway employee, volunteered to try and set the points.

A ladder was put up behind the signal box. Schofield managed to climb unseen in the dark and get in a window. He crept stealthily along the floor of the box and reached the levers. Bricks and boiler rivets were still flying through the air with dangerous regularity as Schofield bravely made his way back.

Now that the points had been adjusted, the trains had to be alerted. Station employees did not care for the job and so the stationmaster came up with a plan. He borrowed a hat and coat, to hide his uniform, walked across the street unrecognised, and then notified the police to be ready while he signalled the trains to start.

They began to shunt through at 10.10pm under a hail of fire when two young men from the crowd surged forward, released the bolts, and banged the gates shut again, right into the path of the approaching train. The men were struck hard on their heads by police and dragged out of the way. The line was cleared just as the train reached the road. It would have been impossible for it to stop.

A fragment of brick flew through the air and struck a police notice board near the High Street Conduit, by St Mary Le Wigford Church. People scattered. No-one knew where the ammunition was coming from. Cheers followed every successful shot. One man tinkled a bell every time a pane of glass was hit and offered a cigar or coconut to the person who threw right on target.

A missile from the north side of the crossing came from an unseen hand and struck PC Henry Capes on his temple, felling him like a log. His helmet saved him and he resumed duty despite concussion. Police Sergeant William Skelson was hit so hard with a piece of coal his chain went through his helmet.

Another missile hit Chief Constable Coleman in the back and during the violence that followed, several innocent people in the crowd were injured. Casualties included a woman who had to be taken to the station for treatment and a child who was cut over his eye.

There were still hundreds of troublemakers present at midnight. By 12.30am Coleman had left the scene and this seemed to herald the beginning of the end. Some of his principal officers went with him, but hundreds of people from the crowd followed, acting as his unnecessary escorts, booing and calling out scathing epithets all the way up High Street and Silver Street to his home at the Sessions House on Lindum Road.

Once he disappeared from view, the crowd began to fall away. By 1am, the police dispersed and the last of the stragglers began to think of bed.

Police Officer on guard at Railway crossing.

Hooligans trying to coax police away from their post (Note the man at the gate hooting at the officer).

People drifted to the railway gates to support the strikers

Police board a waiting train ready to escort it through the gates

Railway Inspector who came up with a plan to get the gates open

CHAPTER TWO
Best laid plans....

AUGUST 19 and 20, 1911. High Street, and the Midland Station, St Mark's Street. 7pm to 1am.

The City authorities reacted to the trouble by calling a meeting. The Mayor Mr C.H. Newsum, the Watch Committee Chairman Alderman Hugh Wyatt, the Town Clerk Mr W.T. Page, Chief Constable Coleman, and the Deputy Clerk to the Magistrates were present.

The Home Office instructed that Special Constables should be enlisted but Coleman said that despite efforts to find 50 volunteers only four were recruited in time for the start of the railway strike.

This was holiday season in Lincoln and many people were away including the Clerk to the Justices Mr E.E. Tweed who was in Conwy, North Wales. No-one seemed sure of what the duties of the magistrates would be in the event of further disturbances. The Deputy Clerk consulted his text book and told the meeting he would find out.

Coleman was instructed to bring in extra officers, alert the military to be ready in the event of another outbreak of violence, and arrange for a magistrate to be present to read the Riot Act which would give the soldiers the authority to restore order if necessary.

The City hoped that if trouble broke out again, there would be 56 police from Lincoln, 30 from the County Force and 80 soldiers stationed at the barracks on Burton Road.

Newsum, City Mayor and Chairman of the Magistrates' Bench, was in Lincoln for the day to open the Co-operative Society's Jubilee Exhibition at the Drill Hall on Broadgate.

He appealed to the "cool, level headed, working men" to stay off the streets because if their cause was just it would not be benefited by a breach of the peace. "I want, if at all possible, to say that such disturbances as I understand took place last night ought not to be repeated in the City of Lincoln, a City with such fame as we have," he said.

Despite the risk of a further night of trouble, Mr Newsum did not stay. He returned to his holiday in Sutton on Sea saying his wife would be alarmed if he was caught up in the trouble.

Coleman contacted County Force Chief Constable Captain Cecil Mitchell-Inness and was promised extra men. At 7pm he contacted the Officer Commanding the Troops, Major Fitzgerald Cox, to ask that his men be held in readiness. At 10pm, he went down to the Stonebow. All was quiet in town so he went back to the Sessions House.

At 10.40pm Major Cox sent his adjutant to enquire from the Chief whether soldiers would still be needed. Coleman was "resting" when his adjutant arrived.

"The adjutant, however, insisted on seeing the Chief Constable and he eventually appeared in a state of dishabille," Major Cox said. "He informed the man that there was no fear of a riot and that the military would not be required."

Major Cox sent his men to bed.

There was still not the slightest indication of any disorder by 11.30pm on the Saturday night. The stations were closed and the trains diverted. The mail, which was carried along the Avoiding Line, was collected after being thrown from the iron railway bridge near Gowt's Bridge.

The previous scene of trouble, the Great Northern level crossing, was deserted. There was a ghostly feel about the place. Pickets and railwaymen had avoided the area knowing that the stations were to be shut at 6pm. There was nothing for them to gain from being in the City Centre.

There were three officers in the area under command of Inspector Milner from the Central Police Office. A group of "mischievous imps" was pelting stones and watching them roll down a slated roof. The officers approached warily, watching out for offenders. A young fellow was seized and arrested. Instantly the officers were attacked. They stuck to their man and walked him swiftly through the street but a fast gathering crowd followed. The High Street exploded in a scene of utter disorder, Roughs and hooligans poured out of the side streets, accompanied and egged on by red faced screaming women who surrounded the three officers with threats while pelting them with stones they carried in their aprons.

A company of City Police approached and seeing what was happening they made a charge on the group. Someone shouted: "Now lads, we've got 'em" and a general commotion followed. Police and mob were mixed up indiscriminately, fighting and struggling, pushing and shouting. Pandemonium was let loose and it seemed to the people of Lincoln that all the devils in Pandora's Box had been set free. And then began the crash of glass which was to hang on the humid air all night.

Every now and then a cheer roared out as another large square plate had been staved in.

The event appeared to be pre-planned. People came prepared for violence. One man had a string of bottles around his neck, taking one out every now and then from his "barbarous bandolier" to fling it at either a window or a policeman.

Gangs of youths and young men began to work at various points of the street, watching for opportunities to smash more glass, bring down electric arc lamps and fuel terror with darkness. What could happen under the secrecy of dim lights was in everybody's mind as the lamps steadily continued to smash. The police were utterly helpless.

It was felt that the mob had been conjured into being and the police lured into a trap because nothing but a premeditated plan could have mustered so much raging disorder within a matter of a few minutes.

Messages were sent for further contingents. Every available city constable was summoned to duty but the Force was hopelessly outnumbered. Instructions from the Home Office to take on special constables to help strengthen the City Force were ignored, and therefore lack of manpower meant that attempts to clear the crowd were futile.

Reinforcements arrived in the shape of the County Force. Its officers had been lying in ambush just outside the City boundary at Boultham. There were rumours of an attack there but this never materialised. By the time Captain Mitchell-Innes' men arrived to assist the City men in High Street, violent disorder had reached an alarming pitch.

Stones, bottles and bricks flew across High Street. Windows literally fell out. Women shrieked. Flushed and flaunting "viragoes" stood on street corners urging on the rowdies and informing them of the movements of the police.

"Smash that bugger, Bill" and "Stave that one," was followed by the breaking of glass and the cackling laughter of the Waterside Women.

The City was in absolute chaos. Joining shoulders with the City Force, the County police officers formed a double line in an attempt to clear the streets.

Police advanced slowly but a large mob element, hiding behind the backs of curious spectators, hurled more debris.

The police took the offensive for their own protection and there was no holding them back. They lost all sense of consideration and began to hit out at anything or anyone, beating and belabouring without mercy. The "cracking of heads like walnuts against police batons" went on for "two interminable hours." They managed to beat the mob down. Some people scampered to safety, but the fighting was by no means over.

The crowd responded to the baton charges by taking up the battle again in earnest. Many police officers, Inspector Milner among them, received blows from stones, and there was an absolute shower of missiles flying through the air at the police who stuck to their duty. It was a fearful encounter which left many injured. Every charge left men, women, and policemen groaning and bleeding on the ground.

The City Centre became one long scene of fighting. The noise and shouts, the scampering of feet, and the crackle of broken glass echoed through the night and into the early hours of the morning of Sunday, August 20.

Casualties were carried off constantly. Hundreds sought refuge in St Benedict's Square. People rushed in at both entrances. "Maddened" police officers followed. The crowd hoped to get out by Crown Yard but the gates were locked. Police and mob then met in a terrible impasse with constables at each end of the Square beating down on the struggling writhing heads between. Some of the injured managed to get into the churchyard. Others climbed trees.

The police acted efficiently, pausing only to gain breath before the next charge was sounded by the cheery cry of Inspector Sindell. Further up the High Street hundreds of rioters fled in terror from half a dozen officers with staves, throwing brick-bats and bottles as they went, but as one gang scattered another gathered in its place and another boom and crash told the devil's game they were playing. The same sequence was followed all night. First a howl of rage, then the police's cheery : "Come on lads!" the scurry of feet and the smash and shiver of panes of glass.

Hooligans ran from one place to another and a gang was sent to St Mark's Street. The chilling warning "FIRE!" sounded. Hundreds followed it and joined the general rush in the direction of the Midland Station. Flying down Waterside, down Saltergate, and the Cornhill, Tentercroft Street, the marauders took any avenue to reach St Mark's Street where a general assault on the station was being made.

Already battered, the station, had given up under the sheer force of the attack and now the rioters were concentrating on the offices of Messrs Bass, Ratcliffe and Co nearby.

First the doors and windows were crushed in by the mob and then they gathered up every piece of wood, battering ram and stick. Piled up with other debris in a heap inside the building, it was set alight in the middle of the floor. To ensure it caught well, and as much destruction as possible was caused, hooligans stole the crossing lamp and smashed it through a window. The oil ran, flared up, and the blaze was soon out of control. Yells of delight greeted the tongues of flames darting through the doors and windows.

Employees of the company aided the police in their attempts to quell the blaze and someone ran for help from the City Fire Brigade. In a short time, the fire engine arrived and within a quarter of an hour succeeded in bringing the fire under control. The Midland had been left a burned out shell but while the brigade had been busy, the mob fired other offices on the north side of the line adding to the ever increasing cost of damage.

While the efforts of the Brigade drew with it the attentions of the police, another swarm of men smashed every window in the Great Eastern offices in St Mark's Square, reducing the place to splinters. People who were now acting as crazed savages would have fired that too but, surrounded by dwellings, they were moved by the screams of women from upstairs windows who begged them to stop lest their children be burned in their beds.

In was into this senseless fury that Chief Constable Coleman arrived in his capacity as Captain of the Fire Brigade.

N.B.—This Form must accompany any inquiry respecting this Telegram.

POST OFFICE TELEGRAPHS.

Office Stamp. LINCOLN AU 19

EYRE & SPOTTISWOODE, Ltd., Lond.

If the Receiver of an Inland Telegram doubts its accuracy, he may have it repeated on payment of half the amount originally paid for its transmission, any fraction of 1d. less than ½d. being reckoned as ½d.; and if it be found that there was any inaccuracy, the amount paid for repetition will be refunded. Special conditions are applicable to the repetition of Foreign Telegrams.

Office of Origin and Service Instructions. OHMS Parliament St.

Charges to pay s. d.

Handed in at 3.16 P.M. Received here at 5.17 P.M.

TO { Mayor of Lincoln.

The military authorities have been charged with the duty of protecting the railroads and all railwaymen who continue at work and the General Officers commanding the Various military areas are

N.B.—This Form must accompany any inquiry respecting this Telegram.

POST OFFICE TELEGRAPHS.

Office Stamp. LINCOLN AU 19 11

EYRE & SPOTTISWOODE, Ltd., Lond.

If the Receiver of an Inland Telegram doubts its accuracy, he may have it repeated on payment of half the amount originally paid for its transmission, any fraction of 1d. less than ½d. being reckoned as ½d.; and if it be found that there was any inaccuracy, the amount paid for repetition will be refunded. Special conditions are applicable to the repetition of Foreign Telegrams.

Office of Origin and Service Instructions.

Charges to pay s. d.

Handed in at .M., Received here at .M.

TO {

instructed to use their own discretion as to whether troops are or are not to be sent to any particular point the Army regulation which requires a requisition for troops

Telegram from Home Secretary Winston Churchill instructing City Police & Magistrates to cooperate with the Military (continued over)

N.B.—This Form must accompany any inquiry respecting this Telegram.

POST OFFICE TELEGRAPHS.

EYRE & SPOTTISWOODE, Ltd., Lond.

If the Receiver of an Inland Telegram doubts its accuracy, he may have it repeated on payment of half the amount originally paid for its transmission, any fraction of 1d. less than ½d. being reckoned as ½d.; and if it be found that there was any inaccuracy, the amount paid for repetition will be refunded. Special conditions are applicable to the repetition of Foreign Telegrams.

Office of Origin and Service Instructions.

Office Stamp. LINCOLN AU 19

Charges to pay s. d.

Handed in at .M., Received here at .M.

TO

from a civil authority is suspended the police and magistrat should cooperate in every possible way with the military and it is essential that the police should give assistance in

N.B.—This Form must accompany any inquiry respecting this Telegram.

POST OFFICE TELEGRAPHS.

EYRE & SPOTTISWOODE, Ltd., Lond.

If the Receiver of an Inland Telegram doubts its accuracy, he may have it repeated on payment of half the amount originally paid for its transmission, any fraction of 1d. less than ½d. being reckoned as ½d.; and if it be found that there was any inaccuracy, the amount paid for repetition will be refunded. Special conditions are applicable to the repetition of Foreign Telegrams.

Office of Origin and Service Instructions.

Office Stamp. LINCOLN AU 19 11

Charges to pay s. d.

Handed in at .M., Received here at .M.

TO

guarding the railways and should supply effective protection to railwaymen outside the railway premises

Home Secretary

212,856.

HOME OFFICE,

LONDON.

17th August, 1911.

Sir,

I am directed by the Secretary of State to say that, in the event of a general railway strike or other serious emergency, it will be the duty of each Police Force to give effective protection to life and property and also to all railwaymen within their jurisdiction who wish to work. If the force at your command is not adequate for this purpose, it will be necessary for you to have special constables sworn in, and the Home Secretary strongly recommends that you should take immediate steps to have suitable men ready to be sworn as special constables if necessity should arise. Men of trustworthy character and good physique should be chosen, and in the first instance you should if possible obtain the services of public spirited citizens whose position enables them to serve without pay. You should consider whether you can employ them most advantageously to take the place of constables withdrawn for special duty or to strengthen the police guards at railway stations and other points where disturbance may arise.

Where necessary the Government will contribute one-half of the pay of a certain number of paid special constables up to a maximum pay of 5/- or, if necessary, 6/- for each day of actual duty, provided that the constables be men of good

His Worship
The Mayor of
Lincoln

The Government's offer to pay for Special Constables *(continued overleaf)*

character and thoroughly suited for the work (e.g. police pensioners, ex-soldiers, and others accustomed to discipline) and that the number ofor whom the Government will contribute will not exceed fifty per cent. of the authorized strength of the Force except with the special sanction of the Home Secretary.

I am,

Sir,

Your obedient Servant,

Edward Troup

Extract from Home Sectretary's letter telling the city it had a duty to protect life and property. It instructed that special constables would strengthen the police force. None were enlisted and so officers were 'hopelessly outnumbered'.

Supt. J. Churchill, of Lincoln City Police Force, who to-day completes 40 years' service with the force, is second from the right in the third row of this photograph, taken outside the Sessions House, Lincoln, in August, 1911. Reading from left to right:—
Back row.—P.c.s W. Sufton, I. L. Lunn, J. Wright, A. E. Taylor, C. W. Brumpton, T. F[illegible], [illegible] Walker, A. K. Wills.
Second row.—P.c.s A. E. Lilburn, G. W. Jackson, J. W. Wrench, S. Flowers, C. A. Fox, J. J. Allen, C. Houghton, T. H. Cook, F. Borman, C. W. Bryan, C. T. Cook, J. Bailey.
Third row.—P.c.s J. O. Taylor, S. Limb, W. H. Ash, W. Bass, H. Cawkwell, J. Chapman, Det.-Segt. G. Brierley, Sergt. D. Dunglinson, Sergt. W. H. Skelson, Det.-Con. G. Wallhead, P.c.s J. T. Seymour, J. Brown, J. Churchill, J. W. Clarke.
Fourth row.—P.c. D. Wright, Sergt. A. G. Froggatt, Sergt. J. Cook, Sergt. T. Bell, Insp. F. Milner, Chief Constable J. T. Coleman, Insp. T. E. Culpin, Sergt. F. Andrews, Sergt. A. Vessey, Sergt. G. E. Capes.
Front row.—P.c.s J. F. Brown, F. W. Rowe, A. Bens[illegible] T. Elsey, C. Dobbs, H. Capes.

City Police Force

The smashed up Eastern Offices in St Marks Square

Above are the windows where women screamed in fear.

Smashed windows at the Labour exchange

Major Newsum appealed for calm before returning to the bracing air of the East coast and his holiday

O. H. M. S.

LINCOLN 9.15 AM AU 18 11

The Mayor

of the ~~Borough~~ City of

Hartford Lincoln

Sutton on Sea

HOME OFFICE.

Telegram which was forwarded to the City Mayor at his holiday address in Sutton on Sea urging the city to be prepared

CHAPTER THREE
"BRING THE BUGGER OUT - WE'LL MURDER HIM!"

August 20 , 1911. St Mark's and the Stonebow. 1am - 2am.

There was no doubt in many people's minds that the fire had been set for one purpose – to bring out Coleman. Instead of leading his men at a time they greatly needed direction, he sought cover in the safety of the Sessions House. People thought he was a coward but he preferred to risk misunderstanding rather than unduly incense the mob with his presence.

He knew much of the rioting was directed towards him and so he thought it better not to take charge of the proceedings that night for fear of antagonising the crowd further.

Cries of : "Bring the bugger out – we'll murder him!" and "Where's the Chief, he's the one we want to put through it," must have reached his ears.

Now, as head of the Fire Brigade, he was at the centre of trouble. He had no choice but to come out of "hiding."

Coleman took PC Alfred Clay with him to the scene hoping that his presence would quell the rioters. Clay, who was also a fireman, was a lay preacher and President of the Lincoln and District Christian Endeavour.

However, an outburst of malice assailed Coleman as soon as he arrived. Abuse, threats and disgusting language was hurled at the Chief Constable. Stones rained on him and now and again came an ugly rush which was only thwarted by the steady determination of the police.

There could be no misunderstanding. The threats to murder him were real. It is down to Coleman's coolness and the courage of his men that he escaped without serious injury. He neither flinched nor retaliated but, white as death, he took in the sight around him and began to take charge of the situation.

An urgent message requesting military aid was received at the Burton Road barracks at 12.40am – an hour after the riots broke out. The order to "fall in!" was given by Major Cox immediately.

"The men were issued with ball ammunition and left barracks at 1.10am arriving at the Sessions House at 1.40am," Cox said.

"We were directed to the Midland Station and on arrival at this latter place, in spite of previous requests, no magistrate was present, nor did one appear for fully half an hour.

"I may here point out that in the absence of a magistrate to read the Riot Act (except under very grave circumstances, placing great responsibility on the military officer in command) soldiers can take no action. It is the duty of the Chief Constable to arrange for the presence of a magistrate."

Coleman claimed he had tried to get several magistrates without success. It was holiday season, others did not want to attend, but eventually Dr Mansell Sympson agreed to come.

Meanwhile, the crowd had been stunned into silence by the sight of a company of about 80 men from the Lincolnshire Regiment marching down High Street. Led by Major Cox, DSO, Captain T.D. Gibbes, and Lieutenants J.F. Richardson and P.L. Hammond, they put the fear of God into the hearts of those who saw them. Their appearance had an immediate effect upon the frenzied atmosphere. Caring little whether their actions could be seen as threatening, the Company halted at the Stonebow, the command was given to fix bayonets and the rattle of steel was quite enough to intimidate the mob into submission. The crowd scattered at once and the soldiers advanced in a column with their bayoneted rifles at a slope.

The column spread quickly across the street with the officers in front. They moved quickly, carrying the people before them. There was a visible sense of awe as the armed men took possession of the streets.

Major Cox left his column for a consultation with the Chief Constable at the Midland Station. The conversation was plain and to the point. Cox said he had not come out for show, he was there for business. If it was a question of clearing the streets, he would do it, but he needed the authority.

Half an hour later, Sympson careered through the Stonebow in his motor car. People believed he was carrying a copy of the Riot Act.

He was certainly waving something but it emerged later that it would be impossible to read because no-one had a copy of it!

Pulling up outside the Midland, he talked with the police chief and officers, and then making himself heard as well as he could, he addressed the rioters and explained what reading the Riot Act would mean.

"If there is not an immediate cessation of disturbances, the soldiers will fire upon you," he announced.

"At the sign of the slightest resistance, a whistle will be blown, the police will retire, and the soldiers will charge with their bayonets."

The police lined the street and walked up with the crowd hurrying off before them. The sight of the bayonets scattered the last stragglers. Marching up to the Stonebow, the police were able to leave absolute quiet behind them.

From disorder, the scene changed to utter desolation. At 3am the roads as far as Gowt's Bridge were cleared and by 4am both the police and military were withdrawn.

Chief Constable Coleman was threatened with murder

Smoke pours out of the midland station after a terrifying fire is put out. A mob looks on.

Below: People inspecting the damage caused at the Great Central Railway Gatehouse

The Barracks,
Lincoln,
26th October, 1911.

Dear Sir,

With reference to your letter of the 25th instant I enclose herewith a statement which I trust will give the necessary information as required by the Watch Committee.

Yours faithfully,

[illegible]
Com'd Depot Lincoln.

The Town Clerk,
Lincoln.

Fitzgerald Cox's memo to the Town Clerk about his statement which is printed over the page

The Barracks,
Lincoln.
26th October, 1911.

On the outbreak of the recent railway strikes all officers and men of the Depot were recalled from leave.

About 7.p.m. on August 19th a police constable called on me in barracks with a message from the Chief Constable requesting that the Military might be held in readiness as trouble was anticipated in the City during the night. Consequently all men were confined to barracks and the necessary orders issued in anticipation of a call in aid of the civil power. "Lights out" sounded at the usual hour (10.15.p.m), but the men were told to hold themselves in readiness to turn out. Under my instruction at 10.40 p.m. the Adjutant called at the Sessions House for the express purpose of ascertaining from the Chief Constable as to whether there was still any likelihood of the military being required. He was informed that the Chief Constable was resting. The Adjutant however insisted on seeing him and he eventually a peared in a state of deshabille. He informed the Adjutant that there was no fear of a riot and that the Military would not be required. The Adjutant returned to barracks via the High Street, but not in company with the Chief Constable. At 12.40.a.m a constable arrived in barracks on a bicycle with a message from the Chief Constable requesting military aid. I sounded the "fall in", the men were issued with ball ammunition and we left barracks at 1.10 a.m. arriving at the Sessions House at 1.40.a.m. We were directed to the Midland Station and on arrival at this latter place, in spite of previous requests, no Magistrate was present, nor did one appear for fully half an hour after the arrival of the military. I may here

Statement from Fitzgerald Cox stating that the Chief Constable was in a state of dishevelment (continued over)

point out that in the absence of a magistrate to read the Riot Act (except under very grave circumstances and circumstances placing great responsibility on the military officer in command) soldiers can take no action. It is the duty of the Chief Constable to arrange for the presence of a magistrate.

Before leaving the Midland Station that Sunday morning to return to barracks I was informed by the Chief Constable that there was every chance of a recurrence of riots on that night. I therefore informed him that I should have a guard at each of the town railway stations and I again impressed upon him the fact of the necessity of having a magistrate present with the troops. On my arrival about 8.30.p.m at the Midland Station on the Sunday evening I telephoned to the Chief Constable for information with respect to the state of affairs, and again requested the presence of a magistrate none being forthcoming. The Chief Constable informed me that he would let me know when all was quiet, that he was not personally coming out and that he had telephoned for a magistrate. No magistrate appeared on the scene that night. At about 12.m.n I returned to barracks having been relieved by a detachment of the Northamptonshire Regiment.

J. H. Corkran
Comd Depot Lincoln

The sight of the soldiers' bayonets were enough to disperse the crowd

CHAPTER FOUR
COUNTING THE COST

Sunday and Monday, 20 and 21 August, 1911. City Centre.

Sunday morning dawn revealed the main thoroughfare looking like a battlefield. From the Great Northern Station to the Stonebow was one sickening patch of blood which had to be decently cleaned up in case the general public was offended by the sight on its way to Church. By the time astonished citizens rose from their beds there were only traces of the previous night's orgy left.

Charred buildings and broken windows couldn't be washed away. Mr A Clements' baker's shop had been the first to be attacked. People said he incurred the wrath of the rioters because he refused to subscribe to the Strike Fund and allegedly said that the strikers were idle and worthless men. However, Mr Clements had supported the Fund and he was in sympathy with the cause. His shop was more likely targeted for the booty it contained.

Looters had then moved on to Messrs Jackson, the hatters, which had been stripped of its goods, but the most audacious assault was on F. Dunn and Sons. People passing by just helped themselves to boots while one man stood a few yards away trying to sell half a dozen stolen pairs. A football had been fetched and the new boots tried out by a gang of girls and boys who tested them by kicking the ball through various windows and shop fittings.

Other places that had windows put in were : Mr Chas Pratt's premises, Messrs Eason and Son, the Capital and Counties Bank, Messrs Freeman, Hardy and Willis, Messrs Jackson and Son, Messrs Dean and Dawson, Wyatt and Hayes, W.B. Cheer, R.S. Burns, Mr F. Clarke Coal Merchant, the Gatehouse, The G.N. Goods Receiving Office, the Labour Exchange, the G.E. Offices, Mr E.S. Rose Music Warehouse, Bainbridge and Sons, The London Furnishing Company, Messrs Mawyer and Collingham, Mr Leachman's, Stonebow, Lincoln

Rubber Company, High Bridge Vaults, Mr Holdsworth's, High Street, Earl's, Guildhall Street, Miller's, Doughty, Son and Richardson's, Harrison's, Guildhall Street, City Hotel, Cornhill, Gambles, Newmarket, Peacock and Wilson's Bank, Messrs Pennell and Sons, Messrs Foster, Messrs Clipsham, Payne, and Willows, the Albion Hotel, M. Ashley, Manners and Burton, Singleton and Co, Messrs Wallis Bros, Home Yeast Co, Treaty of Commerce Pub, Adam Spencer, Lion Hotel, Great Northern Tap, Neale T. Winter, T.A. Swallow, Melton Bros, the Lindsey Police Office, C. Harrison, Choice and Murfin, Hunter's Stores, and the Great Northern Goods Offices. Seventy gas and twelve electric arc lamps were also destroyed. Damage was put at £1,500.

The full extent of those on the casualty list was never known. There were plenty of people who were careful to hide their injuries for fear of being arrested as troublemakers. Many innocent people were hurt but there was no sympathy for them. Police said arrests would have been made if curious spectators had not got in the way.

"Hundreds" injured was the estimate given at the time and was based on the hours spent banging heads with batons after the police lost control. Many people carried in their minds the sight of men and women running from them with blood streaming down their faces.

Dr F.S. Genney told how he saw the firing of the Midland Station and went to try and stop the incendiaries. He was greeted with laughter and derision but there was no mirth when he was bandaging the heads of several patients who came to him for treatment the next morning. Another medical man, Dr Clements, reported that he saw one of the hooligans deliberately kick in a window at Dunn's. He seized him with the intention of taking him to the police, but he was rounded upon, stoned, kicked and so mauled about that he was "somewhat seriously damaged." He was, however, well enough the resume his professional duties after resting for the day.

There were 16 members of the St John Ambulance Brigade who dealt with 20 cases. Five were taken to Lincoln County Hospital, where one was detained. Dr Hewatt and Dr Macfarland were called out to the Central Police Station which was used as a receiving hospital. They were kept hard at work all night.

Official injuries were listed as : Thompson, Carr Street, cut face. Holdsworth, Rasen Lane, cut scalp, H. Clarke, Newport, cut scalp,. Mrs Barnes, (no address) concussion. Fogg, Drake Street, cut face. Binks, Carholme Road, injury to back. Hutchinson, Eleanor Street, cut face and concussion. Gibbs, St Swithin's Square, injured right arm. Kerrigan, Thorngate, cut head. H Mead, Robey Street, cut head. Noel Sedgewick, Baggeholme Road, scalp wounds.

Serious injuries were also sustained by the police. PC Green was struck a crushing blow with a beer bottle and knocked senseless. He was taken to the Central Police Station. PC Rowe followed in the same condition.

PC Lilburn was given a particularly rough time. He was separated from his colleagues and surrounded by a gang who knocked him down. He came out of the melee full of bruises with a badly damaged nose. His helmet and staff were stolen.

When officers from the County Force were slowly clearing up High Street they came across an army of youths with a young outlaw at its head. He was wearing the stolen helmet and brandishing the baton. Prompt action was taken and the leader received a thrashing he would never forget.

PC Capes and PC Taylor received "nasty hurts". PC Jewells was so seriously kicked and beaten he had to be retired on a pension. Not one member of both forces escaped without some kind of injury.

It was a bitter lesson learned. Contingents of the Lincolnshire Regiment were drafted into the two Lincoln stations on the Monday and were joined by 150 men of the Northamptonshire Regiment, under command of Major Little. They were placed at various parts of the town. Constables were also on duty in full strength from both the City and County forces. They wisely kept in pairs or threes.

With such a guard it seemed foolish for the hooligans to try again. Nevertheless, the same eerie evening silence was met with the same gathering force of crowds in a highly agitated mood. Anything could have set them off. No one knew what would happen, but it fizzled out to nothing. The gangs thought better of trying to battle with armed soldiers and gradually faded away. By midnight the streets were deserted.

Railwaymen, who were keen to distance themselves from events, publicly announced that : "We the Railwaymen of Lincoln, deeply regret what took place on Saturday night. We are fully convinced this was not taken part in by any railwayman."

Labour delegates representing a large body of organised workers in Lincoln, including the boilermakers and gasmen, protested against Chief Constable Coleman's actions in "overstepping his duties and interfering with a perfectly orderly Labour demonstration on August 14," and wrote to the Home Secretary, the Chairman of the Watch Committee and the press.

"Such unseemly and uncalled for action as the breaking up of the men's banner by constables, obviously under orders from their Chief, is at such times eminently calculated to exasperate men to a breach of the peace.

"We further protest against the unwarrantably provocative attitude of Chief Constable Coleman which we consider was directly incentive to riot and disorder and we attribute the whole of the disorder occurring on the 18th and 19th to his actions."

This group certainly didn't deny being involved as strongly as their railway colleagues had done, but whether the police came to their arrests after talking to their members, or whether the City Corporation reward of £25 flushed out the guilty, is not known. However, by the end of the week, 12 men were singled out as ringleaders and remanded to appear before the magistrates' court.

F Dunn & Sons suffered the most audacious assault of the evening and rioters helped themselves to boots after smashing up the place

Armed guards from the Northamptonshire Regiment on duty at the Great Northern Station

Northamptonshire soldiers taking a break in the shade from the stifling heat of turbulent Lincoln in August 1911

Sir. I have the honour to point out the
following for your information.

At present the troops at Lincoln are
placed as follows:—

½ Company at the Midland Railway Station
under an Officer.

½ Company at the Great Northern Railway
Station under an Officer.

Remainder of troops, Lincoln Depot and one
Company, 1/Northamptonshire Regt., at the
Barracks, Lincoln.

2. At neither of these places is a Magistrate
in case it might be necessary to read the
Riot Act and this omission might cause
serious delay should the troops be required to
Act.

I request, therefore, that this may be
remedied as soon as possible.

Kindly acknowledge receipt of this letter.

I have the honour to be
Sir,
Your obedient Servant
J. Latto. Major
1/Northamptonshire Regt.
O.C. Troops

Letter from Major Little to the to the Mayor complaining that a magistrate was still not present

Aug. 21st 1911

Sir

In the Mayors absence from Lincoln he has asked me as Town Clerk to deal with his official Correspondence

I beg to acknowledge the receipt of your communication of todays date

At a Meeting of Magistrates held yesterday Dr. E. Mansel Sympson J.P. of Deloraine Court, James Street Lincoln undertook to hold himself in readiness to read the Riot Act should necessity arise

I will however bring your letter to the attention of the Chief Constable and Justices Clerk with a view of providing additional Justices to deal with the matter should emergency arise

I am Sir
Your obedient Servant

To Major J. Little
Officer Commanding Troops
The Barracks Lincoln

A reply to Mayor Little saying magistrate Mansell Sympson was ready

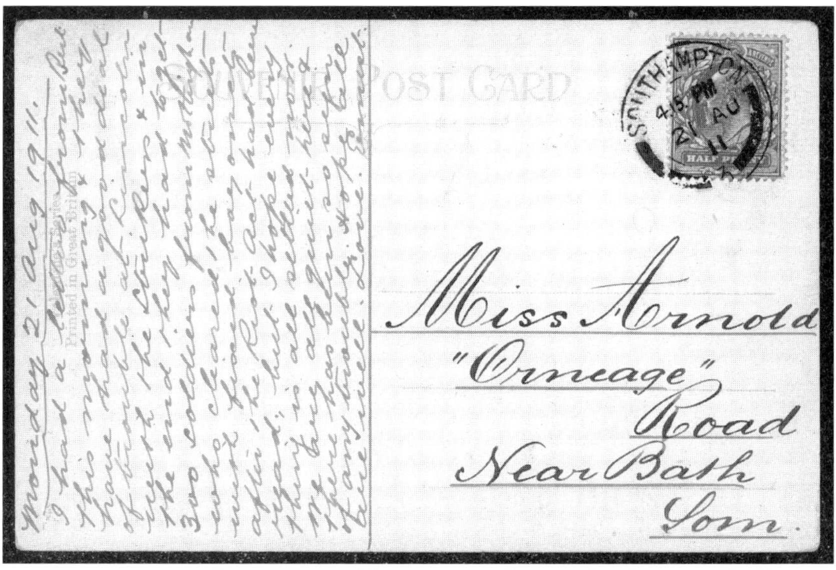

A contemporary postcard to a 'Miss Arnold' in Somerset telling her that the Riot Act had been read after "A good deal of trouble in Lincoln"

CHAPTER FIVE
"BROUGHT TO BOOK"

Wednesday and Thursday, August 23rd and 24th, Princess Street, off High Street, Lincoln and The Sessions House, Lindum Road, Lincoln.

Someone had to be punished for causing something that justifiably caused so much public outrage and brought the City to its knees. The police seemed pretty convinced that they knew who was responsible. On Wednesday, August 23rd, they moved in on the addresses of twelve men.

But if the authorities thought that the arrests were enough to bring peace to the City they were wrong. Another riot broke out overnight as the suspects languished in the cells. Whether it was related to their arrest is not known but the consequences were tragic.

A fire at Messrs Osbourne and Bros Motor Factory in Princess Street was reported at 11.20pm on August 23. Fireman Alfred Clay and other officers arrived but they were beaten back by flames. The cause of the blaze was not determined but it was made worse by the amount of oil on the premises.

Police waded up to their waists in mud to get to the deeper water of the Witham while a huge mob looked on, shouting abuse. Hoots and cheers hailed the shortage of water. Bricks were flung at the police and firemen to hinder their efforts in quelling the blaze that threatened to burn down neighbouring homes. Women screamed in fear that they would be homeless.

After several frantic efforts, firemen managed to fix the hydrant to a point on High Street. They battled with the blaze for an hour and a half and eventually brought it under control, saving neighbouring properties.

Clay (38), who stood shoulder to shoulder with Chief Constable Coleman during the terrifying fire at the Midland Station just a few days earlier, was checking that all was clear as the flames began to die down. A crowd surged forward. He ordered people away from a wall that looked ready to collapse. Local tradesman Mr TH Starmer, a picture framer of High Street, urged the mob to let him get on with his job.

Starmer held Clay's ladder to the wall as the fireman climbed up to look inside the charred building and ensure that no one was trapped. There was a huge crash. Both men were buried in rubble when the wall fell. The mob stood back as they were pulled clear. Clay was taken to the house of labourer, Mr Thomas Brown, at 25 Princess Street, but he was badly crushed. There was no hope. His body was taken home to Rosemary Lane and his widow fainted at the sight.

Mr Starmer was taken to Lincoln County Hospital by the St John Ambulance Brigade. He suffered a fractured skull and died the next day.

Feelings were running high by the time the accused rioters appeared in court the morning after the fire. More than 100 people crammed into the public gallery.

The defendants were lined in a double row in the dock. Their names were read to the court :

Frederick Wright (24), labourer, of 6 Providence Cottages, Lincoln.
Frederick Goodwin (16), labourer, of 11 Swan Street, Lincoln.
Arthur Wadsworth (41), labourer, of 25 Henley Street, Lincoln.
Albert Brewitt (45), labourer, of 10 Lytton Street, Lincoln.
George Salmon (22), labourer, of 59 Westgate, Lincoln.
Arthur Abey (33), fish merchant, of 30 Sincil Bank, Lincoln.
Noel Sedgewick (32), labourer, 54 Baggeholme Road, Lincoln.
Arthur Tayles, (16) drayman, of 21 Thesiger Street, Lincoln.
Luke Goates (25), labourer, of 27 Charles Street West, Lincoln.
Frank Cammack (26), moulder, of 39 Eastbourne Street, Lincoln.
Frederick Elsom (20), labourer, of 34 Stamp End, Lincoln.
Charles Logan (33), labourer (no address recorded).

There was an audible gasp as the men appeared, bruised, and many with their heads swathed in bandages, but there was no sympathy from the bench.

And then in the antiquated language of the law, the charge, within the meaning of the Summary Jurisdiction Act, 1879, was read :

"That between the 19th and 20th days of August, 1911 inclusive, at the Parish of Lincoln, together with divers, other evil disposed persons to the number of one thousand and more, unlawfully, riotously, and routously did assemble and gather together to disturb the public peace, and then unlawfully, riotously, routously, and tumultously did make a great noise, riot, tumult and disturbance, so to the great terror, alarm and disturbance of His Majesty's subjects there being and residing, passing and repassing against the peace of our Lord, the King, His Crown and Dignity."

Councillor C.H. Newsum, the Mayor, presided over Messrs R. Hall, J. Richardson, S. Bainbridge, H. Wyatt, F. Clarke, W. Rainsforth, G. Bainbridge, W. Watkins, W. Mortimer, E. Harrison, J.S. Battle, and C.W. Pennell on the bench.

Mr W.T. Page, Town Clerk, prosecuted, and Mr H.H. Williams defended Tayles. The other prisoners were not represented.

Mr Page said he would prove that the defendants were present on that Saturday night and that each one was a party to violence. He called upon others who had been involved in that, and other disorders, to heed the lesson that these 12 men were now learning.

"It is a great satisfaction to us, and I believe the citizens at large, that the police have been able to place their fingers upon a considerable number of those who took part in that riot and bring them to justice so that it might be known by them, and others who took part in such proceedings, that the law is superior to violence," he said.

Chief Constable Coleman was the first to give evidence. He said he reached the Midland Station about 1am and stayed until about 3.30am. He saw very large numbers of people congregated at different points, old, young, men, women, girls and boys.

"Their behaviour was devilish and diabolical. They acted as devils let loose," he said as he described the orgy of the Saturday night and the attacks on police.

"And who were the violent threats against?" asked Mr Page.

"Me, in particular. They were going to murder me, burn me, tear my guts out. I took all of this right up to about 2-2.30am – up to when the military arrived."

"I was with PC Clay..."

At this point, to everybody's surprise, the firm and steady demeanour crumbled. The Chief Constable's voice shook and he broke down, utterly shaking with sobs and groaning: "Oh dear, oh dear."

The sight of this strong man so bitterly moved and pathetic softened the atmosphere of the court and the magistrates showed him a keen sympathy.

"Sit down and wait a moment before resuming," said Newsum.

"No, no, it's fine," the Chief responded sniffling.

"It's just that, as the poor chap is dead, the suggestion of his name got over me. I really can't help it."

He broke down again.

"He would not let me go out by myself, and he stuck to me the whole of the way."

Coleman was given time to recover and then resumed his evidence but was not pressed to go into further detail. He concluded by saying that several members of the Force were injured and one so seriously he would never work again.

PC Arthur Lilburn said he saw Abey near the end of St Mary's Street. He threw stones and shouted : "Come on!" Abey said he was there, he got hit, but he threw nothing.

PC John Wrench, Sergeant George Froggatt and PC Jackson all said they saw Brewitt in the doorway of the Hotel Central on Waterside South. He picked up half a brick and threw it at police. Brewitt denied ever having had a stone in his hand.

DS George Brierly said that while making a baton charge past St Mary Street, he saw Cammack throw stones. He approached the prisoner with Detective George Wallhead and found him with his arm raised with a piece of brick in his hand. Cammack said he was "just looking at it."

PC Froggatt said he saw Elsom at the head of a mob throwing stones. He was one of the ringleaders. He described the accused as a labourer but said : "He seldom works."

PC George Jackson said Goates used the threats : "Down the buggers ... we want the f....... chief here ... we'll knock his f...... head off." Goates claimed he said nothing more than : "Be careful Jackson, you'll have someone on the floor."

PC Alfred Taylor and PC John Brown both said they heard Goates on the Friday night calling for the "f...... chief with his feathers."

DS George Brierly said Goodwin was a ringleader. He heard him urging his group to go for the police but the accused challenged his statement saying it was lies.

The allegation against Logan was that he was standing near the

High Bridge between 11.15pm and 11.30pm when he threw a bottle and several stones as the police charged.

"You are making up some good charges and making innocent chaps go through it," Logan said.

"Each time we made a charge we couldn't see your heels for dust," responded PC Froggatt to the great amusement of the public gallery.

PC Charles Brumpton said Logan was one of the worst ringleaders.

PC Liliburn claimed that Sedgewick rushed up to him as he tried to arrest someone for damage to the GN Signal Box.

"Sedgewick threw a hail of stones and said : "You'll not take him!" and then he pinned me against the wall, and wrenched my staff from me. I was kicked and knocked about which obliged me to release the prisoner and seek cover," he said.

Evidence was also given against Tayles who was arrested near the Black Bull. Salmon was seen between midnight and 1.15am running from a baton charge and he threw several stones at the Stonebow before disappearing down Saltergate.

Wadsworth complained at how he had been treated but DC Wallhead told him : "I don't think you got as much as you deserved."

After hearing from several police officers that they had seen the accused in the act of throwing stones, and heard them swear and make threats, magistrates decided that there was enough evidence to commit the accused men to trial at the Autumn Assizes. When asked if they had anything to say in answer to the charge, they all said : "I have nothing to say," except Tayles who said : "I am not guilty, I did not throw a stone," Sedgewick who replied to the warning by saying : "Not just at present," and Wadsworth who said : "I am not guilty, I did not use the language."

The defendants declined to call witnesses except Logan who provided an alibi. A statement from Walter Horton Plumtree, a butcher of Hill View, Hykeham Road, Lincoln, declared that Logan was in his shop until he closed up at 11pm and he stayed until 11.15pm. It meant that Logan couldn't have been on High Bridge at the time stated but the evidence would change before it was put before a jury in October.

PC & Firefighter Alred Clay attended at the midland with Chief Constable Coleman. Despite being a well respected member of the community his presence failed to quell the rioters.

People line the streets to pay their respects to firefighter/PC Alfred Clay who died in the line of duty, August 24th, 1911.

Onlookers watch as Clay's funeral procession reaches the Canwick Road Cemetery

Alfred Clay's coffin is carried by colleagues

Alfred Clay's interment at Canwick Road Cemetery

CHAPTER SIX
"THERE IS ENOUGH EVIDENCE... MORE OR LESS."

Monday and Tuesday October 30th and 31st. The Assizes, Lincoln Castle

Some "rowdies" appeared before magistrates and Watch Committee members Ald Wyatt and Ald Harrison back in August. One prisoner was sentenced to two months' prison for his part in disabling PC Jewells. Others were fined for breach of the peace. The 12 defendants singled out as ringleaders faced the most serious charges, which would be heard during a two-day trial at the City Assizes.

The alleged rioters were to be judged by a jury made up of men from Lincoln who had "every right to feel outraged at what had taken place in their town."

Mr C.E. Dyer prosecuted on instruction from the Town Clerk. Messrs Williams and Sons, solicitors, instructed Mr R.E. Sandilands to defend Abey, Cammack, Goates and Tayles. The other defendants represented themselves.

The Chief Constable repeated what he said at the magistrates' hearing except that this time he did not break down at the mention of his friend's name.

Mr Sandilands rose to cross examine him. Pulling his gown up to his shoulders, he paused, and then demanded to know what precautions Coleman had taken to prevent trouble after the disturbance on the Friday night.

"What time was the military communicated with?" asked Sandilands.

"I asked Major Cox at 7pm to hold his men in readiness," Coleman replied.

"And what time was that order countermanded?" Sandilands asked.

"It was never countermanded," Coleman said.

Sandilands was trying to defend the men by saying the authorities should have taken proper precautions to avoid trouble. But the Judge, Mr Justice Ridley, ruled that the trial was not a public inquiry into the events of August 18th, 19th, and 20th. Coleman was released as a witness.

DS George Brierly was called to the stand next. He said he saw Wadsworth, Wright, Cammack, and Goodwin throw stones, and he heard them using filthy language.

"I had been tapped with a baton and was rubbing my head when you first saw me wasn't I?" Wadsworth asked in cross-examination.

"You got tapped after," Brierly replied much to the amusement of the court which roared with laughter.

"How many police were there?" asked Wadsworth who complained that he had been bedridden for six weeks with his injury.

"A good many," Brierly replied.

"50?"

"There might have been."

"How many people?"

"A thousand."

"And you heard my voice distinctly?"

"Yes, you were too dazed to get away."

The Judge dismissed Wadsworth's evidence as nonsense and said that if he was "collared" that night then he must have been there.

Wright interrupted to voice the point that was said to be common to all men: "I was there too, but I never pelted," he said.

Sergeant George Froggatt stated that he saw Salmon at about 12 midnight near the High Bridge. He was one of the ringleaders. Froggatt said he saw Elsom urging on a crowd of 2000 people. Brewitt was by the Hotel Central throwing stones as police charged.

PC Charles Brumpton said he saw Salmon behaving very riotously near the Stonebow from his position at St Mary Street

"Could anyone see from St Mary Street to the Stonebow when the two streets were as crowded as they were?" Salmon asked in cross examination but he got no answer.

PC George Jackson gave evidence to say that he saw Brewitt and Goates throwing stones at the police with tremendous force while Goates shouted abuse at the Chief Constable. It was put to him that he had it in for Goates.

"You quarrelled with Goates in the past didn't you?" asked

Sandilands but Jackson denied this.

"I used to lodge at his house. We never argued and I only left to get married." The officer continued to deny that he held a grudge against the accused until a witness was brought in. He confirmed that Jackson had said he would get his own back on Goates one day for getting drunk in the house and "rub it in."

PC Arthur Lilburn said he saw Abey throw stones and incite others to riot. He knew where to find him and so arrested him at home the next day.

Sandilands brought attention to public concern at the darkness of the level crossing at night. Lilburn responded by saying that it was light enough for him to see Abey. However, he was forced to admit that he used to wear glasses and he had not had an eye sight test since joining the Force 16 years earlier.

Lilburn's evidence against Sedgewick was that the accused had assaulted him to prevent him arresting someone he had seen causing damage.

The constable said he also saw Tayles stoop down, pick something up and then he heard glass smashing. He ran after the accused and caught up with him on the East Wharf. It was put to Lilburn that when arrested Tayles said: "Oh, no! I've done nothing wrong."

"I believe he has persisted in his innocence since his father bailed him out," Lilburn replied.

After hearing from an independent witness, James Gylee of Portland Street, the Judge pointed out that there was a weakness in the case against 16 year-old Tayles who obviously stooped down to pick up a basket and not a stone. He said as Tayles was only a boy, the case against him should not be pressed. However, the Judge did not take the same compassionate view about 16 year-old Goodwin.
Goodwin claimed he had been near Gowt's Bridge but he had not used bad language and he did not throw stones. "If Lilburn saw me doing something wrong why didn't he arrest me?" he asked.

"You can't walk about with prisoners on a night like that," the Judge replied.

Sergeant James Cooke said he saw Sedgewick inciting others while under the influence of drink.

In the Magistrates' Court, the evidence against Logan was that he was seen between 11.15 and 11.30pm on High Bridge. An alibi had been submitted stating that he was in a shop on Hykeham Road, Lincoln, up to 11.15pm. Now the jury was told he was seen at 11.50pm.

"I believe if Logan and his crowd could have got hold of the Chief Constable they would have lynched him," said PC Clarke.

Logan said he took no part in the rioting and if he had not been arrested he would have been able to call two witnesses to prove it.

"You better call them then," the Judge said.

"I don't know their names and that's where I'm whacked, sir, but if I had been given my liberty after my arrest I could have searched them out. I only went to town that night to buy a few things. I came down St Mary Street into Sincil Street and bought some plums. I stopped to talk to a friend whose name I did not know and then I made my way home. I had to think about my wife and two children rather than riots," he maintained.

Elsom said he was with two young women who he was looking after and he would not have endangered their safety.

"You might have been talking to the women and then gone with the crowd afterwards," said the Judge.

Wadsworth claimed he was quite innocent and knew nothing of the trouble until a County police officer came up to him and hit him on the head: "I was quite confused after that," he said.

Brewitt said he had made arrangements to go mushrooming in the early hours of the morning but the man he was supposed to meet didn't turn up and so he stood around chatting to a man named Sharp.

Sharp gave evidence to say he saw no stone throwing.

"You must have had your eyes shut then," the Judge said.

"I mean, I did not see Brewitt throw stones," Sharp said. "But I did hear glass smashing."

"What do you think broke the windows," said the Judge in a highly irritated fashion. "They don't generally break themselves. Now go away, do."

The Judge suggested that Brewitt's alibis might have been involved in the trouble themselves and dismissed their evidence.

Sedgewick said he was going down Portland Street when he was met by two policemen who struck him on each side of the head. He was taken to hospital. Cooke and Lilburn were the men who hit him. He wasn't doing anything wrong.

"What were you doing out at this time?" asked the Judge.

"I was walking down the street with a friend."

"PC Lilburn says you rescued a prisoner and took his staff."

"No, I didn't, my Lord."

"I suppose that's how you got the knock on the head?"

"No, my Lord."

Wright declined to go into the witness box.

Cammack denied he had any connection with the riots. He picked up a stone "to look at it" after it hit him on the head. Then Wallhead and Brierly came up to him. His case was not helped when Sandilands emphasised that he had never been in trouble before only to be told by the Judge that the defendant had been fined twice for drunkenness.

Mr Dyer in his closing speech said the defence had tried to set up the authorities as the real cause of the trouble because they had not taken adequate precautions to avoid it, and so therefore the offenders should get off.

"This is the argument of "Contributory Negligence" which is just the same as saying that if one goes to bed, leaving the door unlocked, and a burglar comes and is then apprehended in the act of burgling that house, it would be a good defence to say: "I am not guilty because you left the door open." This is not common sense and it is not common law," he told the jury.

"Law abiding citizens are better off at home on occasions of this kind. If one found men without reasonable excuse in the middle of these riotous scenes, they could not complain if acts which at other times would appear innocent assume a very sinister look."

The undefended prisoners were asked to make statements to the jury.

Logan, who had been crying all morning, shed tears freely as he told the jury that he had never been in such a position before.

Salmon said he hoped they would find him not guilty. He had a mother dependent on him and an invalid sister. He hoped they would give him a chance.

Goodwin said he was sorry he was in this trouble. It had been hard for his widowed mother while he was in prison. He had tried to keep himself respectable.

Wadsworth said he had a wife and two children. He was sorry if he had done anything wrong.

Brewitt said he was sorry to be brought before the court and if they would give him a chance he would try to recover.

Sedgewick said he suffered for what he did, but he had done nothing wrong.

Elsom said he was not guilty, and he was sorry it happened.

Mr Sandilands asked the jury not to be prejudiced by their natural indignation at these riots having taken place in their City. They might think that if precautions had been taken earlier, then this would not have happened and the men would not be in the dock.

"Do not let the shortcomings of the authorities, who had a duty to protect the public and the police from violence, weigh against these men. They should not be made scapegoats of persons who, perhaps, did not do all they might have done," he said.

"Although it is unwise, it is not committing a riot for people to go and have a look at it. Most people were curious. For all I know, members of this jury may have been there themselves."

The Judge summing up said there was enough evidence, more or less, to convict the men, except for Tayles who had already been discharged.

City of Lincoln — to wit

The jurors for our Lord the King upon their oath present that [illegible]
Brewitt Frederick Elsom George Salmon Luke Goates
Frederick Goodwin Frank Cammock Arthur Wadsworth
Frederick Wright Arthur Abey Noel Sedgewick
Arthur Fayles and Charles Logan together with
divers other evil disposed persons to the number of one thousand and more to the Jurors aforesaid unknown between the hours of eleven of the clock in the night of the nineteenth day of August in the year of our Lord one thousand nine hundred and eleven and half past two of the clock in the morning of the twentieth day of August in the year aforesaid being then armed with sticks staves stones bricks and other offensive weapons at the parish of [illegible] in the County of the City of Lincoln unlawfully riotously and routously did assemble and gather together to disturb the Peace of our said Lord the King and being so assembled and gathered together armed as aforesaid did then and there unlawfully riotously and routously make a great noise riot and disturbance and did then and there remain and continue armed as aforesaid making such noise riot and disturbance for the space of two hours and more [illegible] to the great disturbance and terror not only of the liege subjects of our said Lord the King there being and residing but of all other the liege subjects of our said Lord the King then passing and repassing in and along the King's common highway there in contempt of our said Lord the King and his laws to the evil example of all others in the like case offending and against the Peace of our Lord the King his Crown and Dignity

A copy of the charge sheet read out at the magistrate's court

And thereupon in the presence of the said accused we took the following Statements on Oath of the persons who were so called as witnesses by the said accused as aforesaid.

Depositions of Witnesses called by the Accused. Charles Logan

The Examinations of Walter Horton Plumtree

taken on Oath this 24th day of August June in the Year of our Lord One Thousand ~~Eight~~ Hundred and ~~Ninety~~ eleven at the Sessions House in the City and County aforesaid, before the undersigned, of His Majesty's Justices of the Peace for the said City and County in the presence and hearing of the said accused who stands charged as aforesaid before the said Justices.

This Deponent Walter Horton Plumtree of Hill View Hykeham Road. Lincoln Butcher. on his oath saith as follows

You had gone out of my shop before 11.15 Charles Logan on the night of the 19th inst. I ~~ka~~ was closed directly after eleven o'clock.

The foregoing depositions of Walter Horton Plumtree were severally taken subscribed and is sworn to before ~~us~~ on the day and year first before written.

W H Plumtree

Richard Hall

~~W M ...~~

John Richardson

A statement from Walter Horton Plumtree stating Logan was in his shop

CHAPTER SEVEN
"No Better Than Savages."

October 31st, 1911.
The Assizes, Lincoln Castle.

Character references were submitted on behalf of the men. It was said that they were not the sort to get involved in riotous behaviour. City firms S&R Horton and Sons, joiners, builders and stone masons, of Portland Street, and Clayton and Shuttleworth's Ltd, both spoke up for Brewitt claiming he was "a good, industrious, honest and willing worker." George Brailsford, a shopkeeper of High Street, said Wadsworth was "straight and honest". JD Newbold & Sons were convinced that Logan "knew nothing to his discredit." And William Probart-Croft, of the Friar's Lane RC School, who had known Goodwin since he was a boy, said it was most unlikely that he could have played any real part in the rioting.

The jury had heard evidence from the police that they knew these men and knew they were involved. They saw them throw stones, heard them swear, make threats, and they had seen them incite the crowd and urge it on. They recognised the men, even from a distance and in poor light, and they knew where to find them afterwards.

But would the jury believe the men who declared that they were just going about their normal Saturday night business? Their only crime was hanging around to watch the disturbance. They were arrested just because they were there. They had done nothing wrong.

The jury retired at 1.34pm and was waiting for the Judge in the courtroom when he returned from lunch at 2.05pm. When the court was fully assembled, the Foreman stood.

"Have you reached a verdict to which you all agree?" asked the Judge.

"Yes, My Lord. Abey and Goates not guilty. Brewitt, Cammack, Elsom, Goodwin, Logan, Sedgewick, Wright, Wadsworth, and Salmon guilty as charged."

Sitting wretchedly in the dock, the men waited for sentence to be passed but the Judge turned away from them towards the public gallery.

"I have made observations to the Grand Jury in ignorance of what the facts were, in an inquiring mind, to find out where the magistrates were that night," he said.

"It is not my duty to criticise how these things were ordered by the authorities of the City, but I cannot understand to this minute why the riot was not stopped two hours sooner.

"I fully believe that a prompt and proper attitude on the part of the authorities would have stopped the riot at midnight. That is my impression.

"I cannot see anything to show why these ruffians were able to go on, and to fight a pitched battle with the police as long as they could. I don't suppose either side could have gone on much longer.

"I don't know how many baton charges there were. There should not have been any. The appearance of the military would have stopped them earlier. However, these are not our affairs. This is what should have been done."

His attention finally rested on the nine anxious men.

"You have been convicted by the jury for taking part in this riot," he said. "Whatever was thought about the way in which it was put an end to, it could not be thought other than it was of a very disgraceful character.

"I suppose you men before me joined in this riot thinking it was a fine thing to do. There is something in the case that makes me think people like you think it is a fine thing to attack the police given an opportunity like that.

"Of course you became no better than savages, you were savages that night.

"You cannot plead in extenuation that the riot was not put a stop to sooner. You could have desisted. I think if this sort of thing is repeated the punishment will be much greater."

The Judge sipped from a glass of water before turning to his notes laid out before him. Then he addressed the defendants in turn.

"Logan. As you have not been on bail and in prison for some time, I sentence you to three months' imprisonment with hard labour.

"Elsom. Your sentence is six months with hard labour. You have enjoyed being at large since being bailed from prison.

"Salmon. Six months with hard labour." The court drew in its breath and then murmuring began. "It would have been nine months if he had been out on bail and not in jail," the Judge snapped.

"Goodwin. Three months with hard labour. You've been on bail.

"Wadsworth. I cannot distinguish between your behaviour and Goodwin's and so your sentence will be three months with hard labour also.

"Brewitt. You've been in jail but you are clearly one of the ringleaders. I cannot give you less than nine months but as you have already spent time in prison this will be reduced to six months with hard labour."

Suddenly a woman in the public gallery screamed : "No, no!" and there was a commotion at the back of the court. "A very easy sentence too!" retorted the Judge.

"Sedgewick. It would have been six months but you've been in jail. Three months with hard labour.

"Wright. Three months with hard labour.

"Cammack. You've enjoyed bail. Six months with hard labour.

"Take the prisoners down!"

As they shuffled their way out of the dock, Brewitt asked for permission to receive a visit from his mother "before going up hill."

The Judge granted this final request immediately.

Lincoln
Oct. 28. /11.

I desire to say that I have known Frederick Goodwin during the greater part I believe of his School days, he having been a pupil in the Friars Lane R.C. School.

He was always a respectful and well behaved boy.

Since he left School I have

Goodwin's reference from St Hugh's School on Friar's Lane (continued over)

frequently met &
spoken to him
& have had no
reason to change
my opinion of him.
I consider it
most unlikely that
he could have had
any real part
in the rioting
of wh. he is accused,
both on account
of his age, and

the good character
wh. as far as I know
he has always
enjoyed.

William Provost Croft.

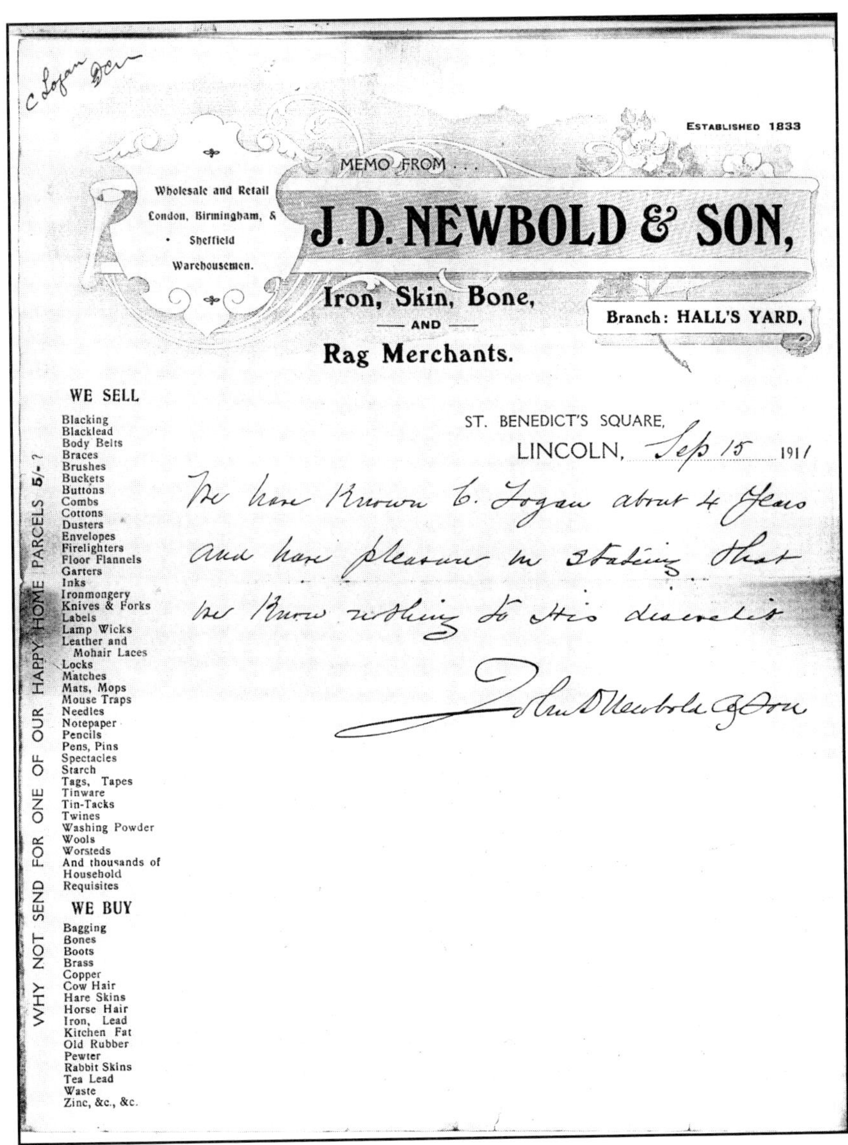

C Logan

ESTABLISHED 1833

Wholesale and Retail
London, Birmingham, &
Sheffield
Warehousemen.

MEMO FROM . . .

J. D. NEWBOLD & SON,

Iron, Skin, Bone,
AND
Rag Merchants.

Branch: HALL'S YARD,

WHY NOT SEND FOR ONE OF OUR HAPPY HOME PARCELS 5/- ?

WE SELL

Blacking
Blacklead
Body Belts
Braces
Brushes
Buckets
Buttons
Combs
Cottons
Dusters
Envelopes
Firelighters
Floor Flannels
Garters
Inks
Ironmongery
Knives & Forks
Labels
Lamp Wicks
Leather and Mohair Laces
Locks
Matches
Mats, Mops
Mouse Traps
Needles
Notepaper
Pencils
Pens, Pins
Spectacles
Starch
Tags, Tapes
Tinware
Tin-Tacks
Twines
Washing Powder
Wools
Worsteds
And thousands of Household Requisites

WE BUY

Bagging
Bones
Boots
Brass
Copper
Cow Hair
Hare Skins
Horse Hair
Iron, Lead
Kitchen Fat
Old Rubber
Pewter
Rabbit Skins
Tea Lead
Waste
Zinc, &c., &c.

ST. BENEDICT'S SQUARE,
LINCOLN, Sep 15 1911

We have Known C. Logan about 4 Years and have pleasure in stating that we Know nothing to His discredit

John D Newbold & Son

City Merchants Newbold and Son stood by Logan

A Brewitt
DC

Stamp End Works
Smiths Dept
20/9/11

Albert Brewitt

I have had this man working under me ~~as Labourer~~ & Striker. He is a good & willing Worker Good Time Keeper General Good all round man. He as worked under me about 16 months

William Peck
Foreman Blacksmith
Clayton & Shuttleworth Ltd
Lincoln

Lincoln firm Clayton & Shuttleworth Ltd. also backed Brewitt

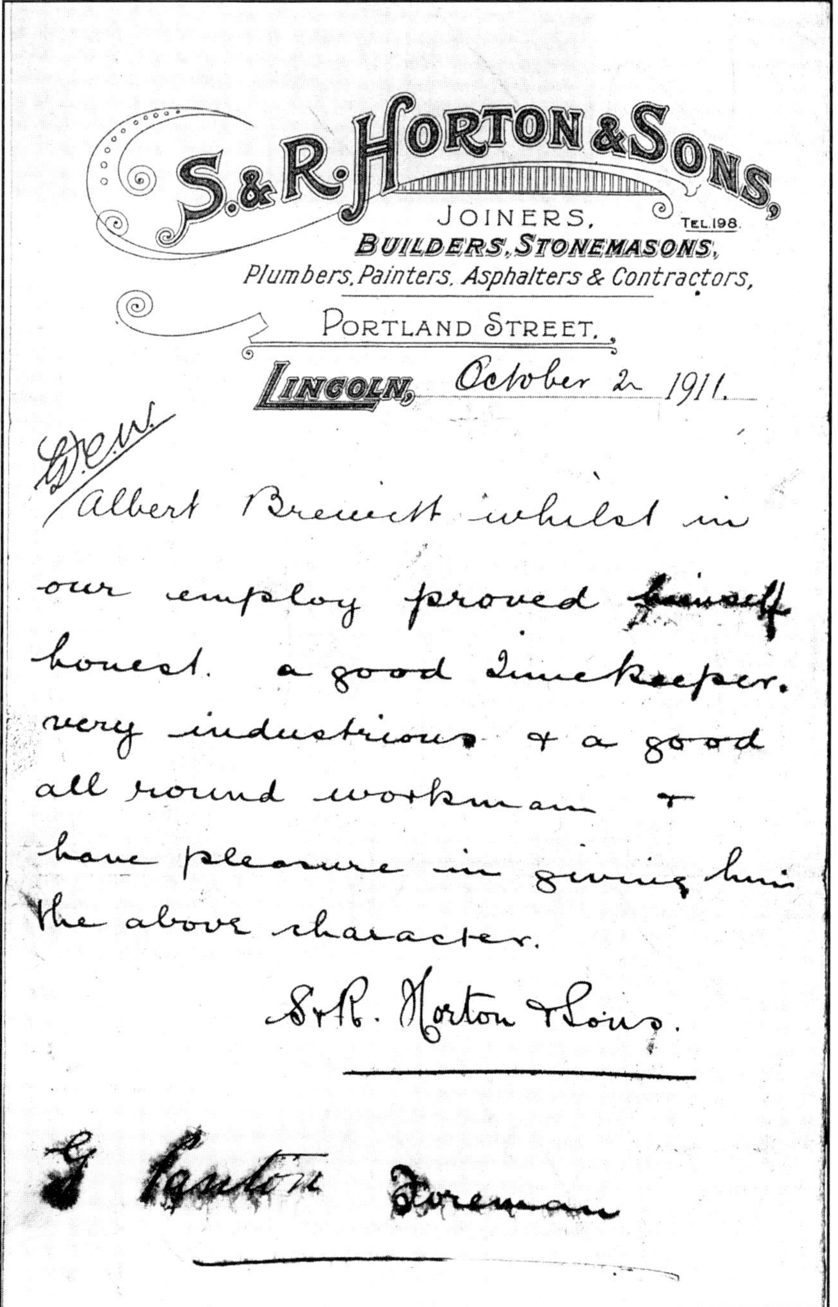

S. & R. HORTON & SONS,
JOINERS,
TEL. 198.
BUILDERS, STONEMASONS,
Plumbers, Painters, Asphalters & Contractors,
PORTLAND STREET,
LINCOLN, October 2 1911.

G.C.W.

Albert Brewitt whilst in our employ proved ~~himself~~ honest. a good Timekeeper. very industrious & a good all round workman & have pleasure in giving him the above character.

S & R. Horton & Sons.

G. Paston Foreman

Horton & Son gave Brewitt a reference

CHAPTER EIGHT
"A VERY GRAVE DERELICTION OF DUTY..."

OCTOBER 29th, 1911 - November 28th, 1911

The Judge's attack on the authorities at the end of the trial was nothing compared to what he said at the opening of the Assizes that autumn.

He began by telling the Grand Jury that there was enough evidence to convict the men, he was sure their alibis were false, and he ended by suggesting that City servants should be indicted for failing in their duty to bring the riot to a swift end.

"There was no Mayor there, no magistrates, nobody to stop it," he said, echoing the citizen's disbelief.

"There seems to have been a grave dereliction of duty, unless they can put forward some reason why they did not do their duty to their King and the Country, and to the citizens."

Ridley's comparison between the similar circumstances surrounding the 1831 Bristol riots, and how the Mayor of that City was indicted for not doing his duty, offended the authorities so much they decided to take action. They boycotted the Divine Service at the Cathedral on Sunday, October 29.

Newsum sent the Judge a message saying that he would not attend the customary ceremony, neither would the City Sheriff, the Magistrates, the Chief Constable, the City Police Force, and there would be no mace bearers.

Ridley was left with a handful of dignitaries to accompany him which included Alderman Edwin Pratt, councillors Milner and Howitt, the High Sheriff of Lincolnshire, Captain J.S. Reeve of Leadenham, and his chaplain, the Rev F.G.H. Knight. There was also a parade of County police.

The authorities wanted to explain to the Judge that they felt adequate precautions had been taken but His Lordship said they should speak to the Press. The affair was featured in both local and national columns which ridiculed the City's incompetence.

The Watch Committee finally compiled a report after months of requests. This stated that the Chief Constable was instructed to have all of his Force at the ready, he was to ask for assistance from the County Force and seek military aid if necessary, take steps to recruit special constables and get a magistrate if one was needed.

It emerged that County Chief Constable Mitchell-Innes had written a "personal and confidential" letter to the Home Office before the riots expressing his concerns at the "utterly defenceless" state of the City Force. He feared its weakness would affect his men.

Sergeant William Skelson spoke up for Coleman in the face of accusations that he was a coward. He said officers begged the Chief not to go out. "From what we heard, we thought his life would be endangered," he said. However, Skelson criticised the officer in command during Coleman's absence. "Several of the men have complained to me of Inspector Milner's conduct and if you ask them you will find that they agree with me that he did seem to show the white feather."

The Watch Committee did look into the allegations made by Skelson and concluded that although it was to be "regretted" that Milner continued in "nominal" command, and remained on duty without rendering any useful service in quelling the riot, he had received injuries, a blow to the head, which accounted for his incapacity.

The Home Office sent down the regional Constabulary Inspector Colonel Eden to look into what had gone wrong in Lincoln. Four days later on November 28, Chief Constable Coleman handed in his resignation.

P.c. A. E. Taylor stated to me that about 11 O'Clock he & P.c E Brown were knocked down by the crowd near the G. N. crossing & they both drew their staffs to defend themselves when Insp. Milner ordered them to put their staffs back. From injuries recd. at that time Taylor had to be taken in the Queen Hotel & soon after had to go off duty.

Several of the men have complained to me of Insp. Milner's conduct during this night & if you ask them you will find that they agree with me that Insp. Milner did seem to show the <u>white feather</u>.

I beg to remain,
Sir,
Your Obedient Servant
W. H. Skelson, Sergt.

J. T. Coleman Esq
Chief Constable

Part of Skelson's letter to the watch committee

CHAPTER NINE
"A MAN WHO DID HIS BEST UNTIL THE TIME OF AFFLICTION CAME.."

DECEMBER 5th, 1911 - The Guildhall

Corporation member Alderman Edwin Pratt was determined to get to the truth of what happened in Lincoln. He raised the riots and the failings of the authorities at the full council meeting on 5th December.

Pratt – who had been one of the few officials to attend the boycotted Divine Service – had compiled a list of discrepancies because of the lack of information supplied by the Watch Committee.

In a circular sent to councillors and the public, he called attention to conflicting information. He demanded to know why Coleman had not gone personally to the barracks to see Major Cox and why both soldiers and police officers were not placed in strategic positions in anticipation of trouble. Why did the Chief only go as far as the Stonebow between 10.30pm and 10.45pm when the chances of a riot breaking out were higher after pub closing time at 11pm? Why didn't the Mayor call a meeting of all Magistrates before leaving the City? Was it true that there was no copy of the Riot Act when a Magistrate did finally turn up?

Also, despite Magistrates saying that there were 56 City Police and 30 County Police on duty between the hours of 10pm and 11pm on the Saturday night, there was, in fact, only a few City Police. No concentration of the Force had been arranged. When the riot was its worst, an officer was sent round to bring men in. The County sent 17 men when requested at 11.20pm and only six or seven more were sent later.

The press and public waited anxiously on the steps of the Guildhall. When the doors opened there was a storming rush to enter. Several hundred people attended knowing that the subject was to be the riots which had culminated in the shock resignation of the Chief Constable. When the question arose of who was to blame for the incompetence, which cost the City financially and also in terms of its reputation, there were cries of: "Name him! Name Him!" The atmosphere was electric when Pratt rose to speak but he did not condemn Coleman much to the crowd's dismay. In fact he paid tribute to a man who had served the City well for 10 years.

"I am quite certain that we have had a very useful man in Chief Coleman. He has always conscientiously tried to do his duty," Pratt said. "I am sure that we part with him with very great regret."

Pratt blamed the Watch Committee who he said had tried to cover up the matter and prevent the public getting full information. "It is now something like 12 or 13 weeks since the riots and this matter has been three months simmering. The reports asked for have not yet been made. I can't help saying it but I believe there is a desire on the part of one council member to smother this matter. The Committee failed miserably in its duty. If it had presented a report to the Council last September, as it should have done, we would never have heard anything else from Mr Justice Ridley."

Alderman Wyatt, the Watch Committee chairman, knew exactly who Pratt referred to when talking about a cover up, but he denied that the report was delayed on purpose saying that it was only the intervention of the Home Office Inspector that slowed things up.

Councillors levelled the accusation that the Committee was out of touch with what was going on in the City. Members did not take adequate precautions to protect life and property. It was said that Magistrates were happy to uphold the law from the safety of their own courts but not at the scene of violent disturbances.

"I live just 10 minutes away and as a Magistrate I was not sought out to bring this matter to an end. Perhaps they overlooked me," Wyatt said. "The rumour that Magistrates would not turn out was false. Only Sympson had been approached. Others were on holiday."

Councillor Scorer said that there was still unrest in the City, yet there was still no plan to deal with trouble should it happen again. Mitchell-Innes of the County Force had said he would not work with Coleman again and until the "matter between them" was cleared up he would not let the City have any more constables. However, had arrangements been made to bring in officers from Sheffield and Nottingham if necessary?

Coleman's letter of resignation resulted from the Home Office Inspector's persuasion that he should retire on the grounds of ill health.

It transpired that he had been under the doctor for some weeks after suffering a nervous breakdown. Everyone in that Council Chamber agreed that resignation was the right course for him to take but the vitriolic malice of some members when discussing his pension was unnecessary for a man who had devoted years of good service.

Coun Godfrey Lowe said the steps taken by the Watch Committee had been "admirable" but the carrying out of their duties was a "ghastly failure."

"Before we decided on the amount of pension we afford Chief Coleman, we should decide whether he was at fault," he said. "If the Chief is guilty of saying something that did not occur, then surely he is culpable and should not receive any award."

Coun Ashley said trouble arose in the first place because of the Chief's handling of a labour demonstration by the Boilermaker's Union. "Let me say, in my opinion, that his actions were very indiscreet. At the same time, the public should know that he was carrying out instructions from the Home Office which I have examined. I can say that the Chief Constable did not exceed his duty, but it is the way things are done that people resent."

Coleman had been treated by the Force doctor, also named Coleman, Some council members thought that in asking him for a certificate of ill health was the same as asking one of the Chief's "working chums." It was also said, however, that Dr Coleman, a professional man, knew more about Chief Coleman's health than anyone else, and so it was perfectly proper that he should issue the certificate.

Alderman Footman said one point had been overlooked. "What view does the Watch Committee take in regard to the disagreement in the accounts given by the soldiers and the Chief Constable?" he asked. "I have no hesitation in saying that I believe the soldiers. However, I do not think the Chief Constable was willingly misleading the Committee or anyone else. The whole of the trouble arose from the prostration and the condition of health of Coleman on that day."

"Whatever has been said, and rightly said, of the Chief's services to the City, his faithfulness and competence in ordinary times, there is not the slightest doubt that events had absolutely rendered him inefficient. They have no right to make a scapegoat of the Chief when the rock bottom of it is the state of his health and nerves on that occasion."

The back of the Hall exploded into mocking laughter on hearing this and there seemed to be no compassion among the public for a man who was once greatly respected.

Coun Milner asked why, if the Watch Committee knew of Coleman's illness, did the members not give him adequate assistance and support?

Ald Wyatt responded by saying that allowances were made. "The Chief was very seriously injured on the Friday night on his legs. He had not slept for a couple of nights and he was not in good form. Bearing in mind what human nature is, one must make allowances for him and as far as I was concerned, all allowances would be made."

Alderman Harris reminded the Chamber that Coleman had been a worthy public servant. "He is a man who had only one object and that was the good conduct of the City and the efficiency of the Police Force," he said. "There never was a more respected man who tried to do his duty more faithfully. Coleman was a man of discipline, a man of nerve, and a man who was worthy in times of crisis."

Brushing aside cruel laughter, Harris said Coleman should not be held responsible for the fiasco and he appealed to the humanity of not only the Corporation but also the citizens.

"It might be your turn to fail next and you might want at the hands of those around you, and the citizens generally, some charitable consideration," he said. "Be as generous as you can and forget the failures of the past and remember him as a conscientious man who did his best until the time of affliction came. Look at the man's good qualities. Do what you can to break his fall which will always remind him of the darkest days of his life."

This speech somewhat turned the feeling of the meeting. Alderman Wallis called for councillors not to turn against a man for making a mistake when he was ill and Coun Robinson urged the City to look to the future.

After agreeing a compromise amount of £175 per year pension – against the £450 annual salary he was getting and the house which came with the post – the matter was finally laid to rest and the authorities set about finding a new man to take Coleman's place.

The ratepayers had been given evidence of who was to blame for the trouble which cost them so dearly, and an unpopular Chief Constable was got rid of to satisfy them. Nine men had paid the price of freedom to teach the citizens not to take matters into their own hands again, two family men had been killed and the City agreed to pay some of the £1,500 damage that had been caused.

LINCOLN RIOTS.

To the Members of the Lincoln City Council.

You will remember that at the Meeting of the Council on the 7th November, I gave notice that at the next Meeting I should call attention to discrepancies in statements of the authorities regarding these riots, and to the absence of explanations needed to clear up certain points.

The statements of the various parties concerned are so contradictory as, in my judgment, call for the fullest and most independent enquiry, and such an enquiry has not yet been made.

As the matter stands, it is impossible to reconcile one with another, the statements made by the Magistrates, by the Military, or by the Police and their recorded reports.

I have chosen to put the following facts before you in print now, in order that you may have an opportunity of leisurely considering them, rather than wait for the next Council Meeting (December 5th), when I should have given effect to my notice.

DISCREPANCIES, &c.

Police and the Military.

Major Cox states in his report, a Police Constable came to him at 7 p.m. (Police say 8 p.m.), and asked that the Military would hold themselves in readiness, as trouble was anticipated that night.

At 10.40 p.m. the Adjutant and another Officer from the Barracks called at the Police Station for the express purpose of ascertaining from the Chief Constable whether there was still any likelihood of the Military being required. The Officers were informed that the Chief Constable was resting. The Adjutant, however, insisted on seeing him, and eventually he appeared in a state of deshabille; he informed the Adjutant there was no fear of a riot, and the Military would not be required.

The Chief Constable denies that he was resting, also denies that he appeared in a state of deshabille, and says he was having his supper. The Chief Constable assured the Watch Committee that he was at the Stonebow between 10.30 p.m. and 10.45 p.m. In cross-examination at the Assizes, the Chief Constable said, the order to the Military never was countermanded. (See Newspaper Reports.)

The Magistrates' Statement to the Judge.

The Mayor, in paragraph 4, states that before leaving Lincoln on the Saturday evening, he personally assured himself that a Magistrate would be in readiness to act if necessary.

Major Cox states, at 1.40 a.m. the Military were directed to the Midland Station, where, in spite of previous requests by him, no Magistrate was present, nor did one appear for fully half an hour after the arrival of the Military.

Note.—It was only after applying to several other City Magistrates that the messenger was directed to Dr. Mansel Sympson, who was called up from bed and taken to the scene of the riots. It was then after 2 a.m., and the Military had been waiting fully half an hour for a Magistrate. The riot ended as soon as the Military made their appearance.

In paragraph 8, relating to Sunday, the Mayor said further, Dr. Mansel Sympson agreed to be in attendance on the Officer commanding the Military for the purpose of reading the Riot Act, if necessary.

Major Cox states that early on that Sunday morning the Chief Constable informed him there was every chance of a recurrence of the riots on that (Sunday) night. He (Major Cox) therefore left a guard at each of the Town Railway Stations, and again impressed upon the Chief Constable the necessity of having a Magistrate with the Troops.

Major Cox states, about 8.30 p.m., that Sunday evening, he again requested the presence of a Magistrate, none being forthcoming. The Chief Constable informed Major Cox he would let him know when all was quiet, that he (the Chief Constable) was not personally coming out, and that he had telephoned for a Magistrate.

No Magistrate appeared on the scene at all that evening.

Pratt's 'Discrepancies ' flyer sent to councillors, press and public

Special Constables.

The Magistrates, in their communication to the Judge, state that on the Saturday morning it was decided that steps should **at once** be taken for the enrolment of Special Constables. This could have been done by the Mayor and Ald. Wyatt or any other two City Magistrates. Previous to the conference between the Mayor, Ald. Wyatt, the Town Clerk, and the Chief Constable, it is reported that a circular letter, dated 17th August last, respecting the appointment of Special Constables, had been received from the Home Office, addressed to the Chief Constable, but I understand that letter has never been presented to the Magistrates or the Watch Committee.

Although Ald. Wyatt stated in the Press on August 23rd, that Ald. Pratt's statement that he did not "fall in" with the appointment of Special Constables was "absolutely false," none were appointed until about 10 or 11 weeks after the riots.

Note.—It should be remembered that there had been a serious riot and destruction of property on the Friday night, and that it was generally reported throughout the City early on the morning of the conference above-mentioned (Saturday) that there would be a recurrence of the riot that evening. Also that two Members of the Council—one being a Member of the Watch Committee—interviewed the Chairman of that Committee (Ald. Wyatt) early the same morning, and impressed upon him that a further disturbance was to be feared, and urged that Special Constables should be appointed, and that Military aid should be available. It is no secret that Ald. Wyatt is not in favour of Special Constables, neither is the Chief Constable. Ald. Wyatt spoke disparagingly of them at a recent meeting of the Joint Standing Committee of Quarter Sessions.

In reference to the Strike in August, the Chairman of the Birmingham Watch Committee (Ald. Sayer) said: "There is an element in this City which is a menace to the inhabitants. If there were signs of this element asserting itself, to the danger of life and property, we should immediately enrol Special Constables, under the powers of the Magistrates to act in a drastic manner."

There was a danger in Birmingham, during the recent Strikes, which few people realised, and it was only by the prompt and effective steps taken to deal with it that prevented a serious outbreak.

The Fire at Messrs. Bass & Co.

In the Chief Constable's own written report to the Watch Committee, relating to the fire at Messrs. Bass & Co., he states that a telephone message was received from the Great Northern Railway Station at 1.30 a.m.

The Chief Constable told the Watch Committee that a telephone call to the fire was received from Messrs. Sharman & Long at 12.45, a difference of three quarters of an hour.

Police Available.

In paragraph 6, the Magistrates state that between 10 and 11 o'clock on the Saturday night there were available 56 City Police and 30 County Police.

Between the hours of 10 and 11 o'clock there were only a portion of the City Police available, no concentration of the Force having been arranged. A Police Officer had to be sent round to bring the men in during the time the Riot was at its worst. The County Police were sent for at 11.20, and arrived at 11.30. At that hour only 17 men were brought, further help was sent for later, and 6 or 7 more County men came. At the date mentioned the City Force did not, all told, comprise 56 members.

In reviewing the whole matter, the following queries suggest themselves to me, as to which the Ratepayers are awaiting an explanation.

QUERIES AND OBSERVATIONS.

Why did not the Chief Constable **personally** interview the Commanding Officer at the Barracks on this very serious matter, instead of communicating with him each time by messenger only?

Did it not occur to either the Officer Commanding at the Barracks, or any of those acting on behalf of the Civil Power, that the Military could not render effective aid in the event of a sudden riot occurring in the middle of the night, unless they were already in a central position, such as the Guildhall, Great Northern Station, Drill Hall, etc., instead of being kept at the Barracks, two miles away, to which there was no telegraphic or telephonic communication ?

Who is **really** responsible for the Military being kept at the Barracks? Did the Magistrates or the Chief Constable expressly request that the Military should not appear in the City unless required for positive action?

Mark the contrast between this and the arrangement by Captain Mitchell Innes—the County Chief—who, on the mere rumour that there would be an attack on the Boiler Works at Boultham, just outside the city boundary, collected from outlying districts an ample force of County Constables, and had them in ambush at those Works, the result being no attack was made. Both in Derby and Nottingham the Military were in readiness in a central position.

Were the Military fully accoutred when they went to their bedrooms, and how far were they prepared to turn out immediately in the event of being called?

Why did the Military proceed by way of the Minster Yard, instead of going the nearest way to the High Street?

Why did the Chief Constable, as he states, come as far as the Stonebow, between 10.30 and 10.45 p.m. on Saturday night, and then return home without going to where the riot had taken place on the previous night, and without staying for closing time of the public houses, after which hour a riot was most likely to occur?

Between what hours was the Chief Constable in bed that night, and why did he not turn out to take command of his men, although he was apprised from an early hour that they were being knocked about and property was being destroyed? It is absurd to suggest that he was incapacitated by injuries received on the Friday night, as he was about the City all Saturday, and turned out to the fire at 1.30 a.m. (Sunday morning).

Why did he inform Major Cox that he was not personally coming out on the Sunday night, although he himself said there was the probability of a recurrence of the riots on that evening.

Why did the Chief Constable, as he states, **walk** to the fire instead of riding on the motor fire engine, seeing that it is his duty, as Superintendent of the Brigade, to get to a fire as speedily as possible?

Why was it not suggested to the Mayor on the Saturday morning that he should immediately call together the City Magistrates, instead of taking upon himself the whole responsibility?

Why did not the Chairman of the Watch Committee call together the Members of that Committee for consultation, as he was in actual communication with more than a quorum of the Committee that morning, each of whom was equally responsible?

Is it true that even when a Magistrate did arrive at something after 2 o'clock on that Sunday morning, the Riot Act could not have been read, as no one present had a copy of it?

Was the Chairman of the Watch Committee, or any other Magistrate, acquainted with the reply of Major Cox (dated October 26th, and sent to the Town Clerk) to enquiries by his Committee, before committing themselves in their statement to the Judge of Assize, on October 30th? (four days later).

EDWIN PRATT.

Lincoln, December 1st, 1911.

CHAPTER TEN
"HISTORY SHOULD NOT BE CENSORED..."

JANUARY 1912 - 2001

Chief Constable Coleman finally relinquished his well paid position of power and honour when he handed over the reins of the City Force temporarily to Inspector Frith from the Metropolitan Police Force on January 1, 1912.

While still in office he reported regularly to the Magistrates. Disorder was still breaking out frequently. An event on Coronation Sports Day, for example, could not continue due to "rowdies" taking control.

"The police were overwhelmed. The crowd did as it liked," Coleman wrote in the Chief Constable's Special File.

Attacks on police also continued. One uniformed officer who was arresting a drunk was suddenly mobbed by a "missiled" crowd and assaulted by women. The officer's clothes were pulled and torn. Things would have gone very badly for him but for a clerk who worked in nearby offices who came to his rescue.

Due to raging disorder, the Premier FA had to close the grounds of Lincoln City Football Club because of hooliganism and the ground remained closed for the first two weeks of the new season.

Coleman was unfortunate in that no Chief Constable before or since has had to endure what he did while in office. He was threatened, mobbed, ridiculed, and the details of his private affairs were held up for public mockery. His reputation as a good and loyal City servant vanished overnight because of poor judgement when he was ill. It is unfortunate that he was labelled a coward. He barely flinched when he courageously faced that mob of people who wanted to kill him. Suffering from insuperable stress, he was constantly on the front line with a poorly resourced Force that was not trained to deal with public disorder on such a grand scale.

The men convicted of taking part in the riots may well have been guilty but they didn't have the benefit of today's high standards of criminal detection and evidence, or a fair and impartial legal system, to remove any reasonable doubt. They may just have been more victims of the turbulence which visited the City in the simmering years before the First World War when young men, described as the "hooligan element", were looking for adventure and a cause to believe in.

For the last 90 years there has been a common belief that railway and factory strikers were responsible for the trouble, which was sparked by the national railway strike, but the authorities at the time doubted this.

On August 21 a notice from the Home Office was pinned on the Guildhall doors announcing that the strike had been settled but trouble continued.

The Government decided against holding a full and independent inquiry into what had gone wrong in Lincoln during August 1911. There was an overwhelming feeling that no good could come from it.

However, questions were barely asked about why the City fathers were so complacent during that summer of intense unrest. Incidents such as attacks on workers during the strikes, battles with the police at public gatherings, and mob violence were common and yet the authorities seemed untroubled. They should have been prepared because what happened during the nights of August 18,19 and 20, had been brewing for months.

The story of the Lincoln Riots is a painful one that has never been told in detail before. We can never ask the main players of the time what their thoughts were, or where they thought the truth lay about who was responsible, because there is no one left who can recall what happened or why.

There are not enough documents left in local archives to compile a true picture without Rabbits' file. Some records are held in the Public Record Office in Kew, Surrey, but locally all that remains is Pratt's Discrepancies Report and a portion of the Chief Constables' Special File with a good chunk of it missing. This was held by Special Branch until a request was made for it to be transferred to the Lincolnshire Police Museum in 1994.

At that time the Force curator noted that the story was of historical significance and that documents should be held in public archives.

A hand-written note on the file stated: "Even though they show the City Force in a poor light, it should not censor history."

Clay's grandchildren say what happened to their grandfather, and the circumstances surrounding his death, were too terrible to hand down through generations. Their grandmother mourned until her death in her 80s and she always wore black. Press cuttings of the fire, the inquest and her husband's funeral were precious keepsakes, which the family only discovered after she died.

Mr Starmer's family must have been in a similar position to that of the Clays. Clay's widow and three children were thrown into poverty at the loss of the family's breadwinner. She was offered 12 shillings from the Police Boot Fund and the chance to put her children in a home. Her 14 year-old son Lewis went to work on the railway instead to support his mother and two sisters.

He had to wait to become a policeman, because only a few were selected each year, but he was determined to follow in his father's footsteps. He joined the Force and the Brigade in 1919 and served loyally and proudly until he retired in 1954.

Clay finally got the recognition he deserved for his bravery and selfless actions when the modern Fire Service and Police Force awarded his grandchildren with the Chief Officers' Commendation in 2001.

The citation reads : "With little regard to his personal safety, Alfred Clay's courageous efforts undoubtedly saved many from injury. The actions of Police Constable/Fireman Alfred Clay were of the highest order and in the very best traditions of the Police and Fire Services."